MAKING MONEY METAL DETECTING

From pocket money to business ideas

REDBACK BOOTH

Copyright © 2017 Redback Booth
All rights reserved.

Created with Vellum

UNTITLED

Keep an eye out for the other books coming SOON in the Redback Booth series!

Like "Redback Booth Metal Detecting" on Facebook to stay updated.

Sign up to the email list for FREE tips, news and updates!

Follow Redback on Twitter ..

INTRODUCTION

Hi! Thank you for reading this book!

I'm nicknamed Redback Booth, and I'm really looking forward to sharing all my tips with passionate metal detectorists like yourself, increasing enjoyment in this great hobby. You can check me out at **Redback Booth Metal Detecting** on Facebook, I'd love to hear from you!

This particular ebook aims to help you make a profit in some way from your metal detecting hobby.

While it's fun to find all sorts of things with our detectors, sometimes circumstances are such that we need to find a way to turn an actual profit. Maybe we are saving for a new detector? Or possibly we need beer and pizza money? Or perhaps we are travelling around the country and want to pay some of our way by indulging in our favorite hobby?

Whatever your reasons for making a profit, this ebook will help give you ideas towards that goal.

My own story of profit is simple. We didn't have a lot of money when our children were young, so spent a lot of time walking them to nearby parks for picnics and family fun. We spent so much time in parks that I felt there must be some way to pass my own time constructively while still keeping a close eye on our children. I had noticed at that point that whatever my children had in their pockets quite often ended up lost in the playgrounds. Matchbox cars for my son, and rings and other jewellery for my daughter would disappear.

So I scrimped and saved and bought secondhand my first ever metal detector - a Bounty Hunter Tracker IV. My first ever find was - you guessed it - a bloody pulltab. But I was hooked from the very first beep!

I found enough money on a regular basis to not only treat our kids to an ice cream, but also to put aside and save for my next detector. This brought me to the question - surely there were other, outside the box ideas for making money from metal detecting?

Over the next decade I collected ideas and tips on metal detecting for profit. I tried out quite a few and had a lot of fun doing my research. I didn't get rich, or make a strong living, but I always had spare change to save for the next detector! I did find a combination of the following business suggestions worked for me rather than just following one type of business in relation to detecting.

This book is the result of all that painstaking recording and research. It's my gift to you!

Things to consider that can erode profits ..

Petrol, parking costs, food and water are all costs to consider. It's best to choose a profitable method of making money from metal detecting that is close to home. For example, I live one hour from the nearest beach, making beachcombing unprofitable for me. I tend to focus on hunting relics in local historical areas I have permissions for, and coinshooting after country festivals, as those are available locally to my home.

I do like to choose holiday locations that are conducive to my hobby, such as gold bearing areas or beach locations.

Quite often I can make enough from my holiday finds to pay for a few good meals out! Once I found a heavy gold bracelet worth $800. After being unable to find the owner, I was able to sell it and fund my next holiday!

Also, there is a tendency among detectorists to keep everything they find .. this is not profitable, unless you're deliberately keeping gold and silver items for peaks in gold and silver prices. It's easy to sell even junk jewellery on Facebook sale groups and online classified sites. Try not to get attached to your finds .. photograph them for your memory archives, then let them go!

1
LOST ITEM RECOVERY SERVICE

This is probably one of the most lucrative ways to straight out detect and get paid for it. Plus the potential for rewards on top of the call out fee!

I remember one lady lost a cherished necklace when her backyard got trenched for drainage installation .. it had great sentimental value. Her backyard was SO trashy! I couldn't ignore the trash signals, as in my experience necklaces can ping up anywhere on the detector ID. I had to go back again and again to try and find it. In the meantime I dug up so much trash .. I did eventually find it and it was worth it all to see her face! She didn't have much money so I didn't charge more than the one call out fee, but man that face was worth so much more than money. Plus she told EVERYONE and I kept getting random call outs to find lost items from people she had told! I still have otherwise hard to get detecting permissions on remote blocks and farms to this day from that one story.

You might need an underwater detector for this one as well as a land detector. Ideally the owner would be able to give you an exact location for where the item was lost, but in reality there's often a fairly large area to cover. This kind of business usually thrives near a beach, as so many items are lost in the sand.

I'd suggest charging a flat call out fee within a certain number of kilometres to cover fuel costs, as well as a recovery fee if a reward amount isn't already offered. Some people charge a flat fee of $100 within one hour of travel for the day.

If on private land, it's usual to negotiate to keep all coin finds as well as the fees. Other items are generally given back to the landowner. This is up to you and the landholder to negotiate. Quite often all the client wants is their item back and they are happy for you to keep anything else found within limits. You might even get permission to detect there forever for yourself!

If on a beach or public area, no negotiation is needed to keep all items other than the recovery item. The same applies in the water. However, it is best to explain this to the client up front so there is clear understanding.

Of course, to be a successful lost item recoverist, you'd need to be skilled at detecting and have a good grasp of geography in some cases. Gridding is definitely recommended for effective searching. Builder's tape and tent pegs are useful for gridding effectively.

Please note that legally, any item of value found other than loose coinage should be handed to police.

If the owner is not found after three months, the item then becomes legally yours to keep or sell. (Based on Australian law at the time of writing - check the finder's law and treasure trove law wherever you are).

You can order cheap business cards and flyers from Vistaprint, or print out your own. Also join all the local lost and found groups or community pages on your Facebook. Handing out business cards is a great icebreaker as well for getting permissions to hunt all sorts of properties. It shows you're serious and not a fly by night who might dig up the property and leave unsightly holes everywhere.

It might be worth putting flyers up nearby on noticeboards, as well as having a Facebook page, and joining up to all the local community Facebook pages and lost item pages as these are where people who have lost items are likely to look. Also keep an eye out on Gumtree, Craigslist and any other online community classifieds for lost notices. It's worth advertising your business on these online sites as well. Drop some business cards off at your local police station. People often go there to find out if someone has handed their lost item in. If I find something locally such as a ring, I put a post up in Facebook community groups saying I'm a lost item recovery service, and I've found a ring, and to message me to describe it to get it back. I got a lot of business out of those types of posts.

Chat with the local surf club, they can refer clients to your business. Call into the local hotels and backpacking hostels and ask if you can leave flyers or business cards there. Join the local metal detecting club, or start one; these are often contacted by clients who have lost items of sentimental or monetary value.

2
BUYING AND SELLING USED DETECTORS AND ACCESSORIES

I have found detecting equipment and detectors at pawn shops, garage sales and online classifieds. I have also put advertisements on online classifieds and on facebook groups advising that I will pay cash on the spot for detecting equipment and detectors.

Knowing the value of the various detectors and equipment is very important.

I aim for a minimum 20% profit margin on lower priced items and 10% profit margin on higher priced items. So a lot of reading and research is needed continually to keep up to the mark on current prices and sales conditions. Generally, high end detectors made me more money but low end detectors sold faster.

It is very important to test the detectors before purchase. Keep an eye out for detectors that have gotten wet at some time and aren't waterproof. These will show moisture or misting on the inside of the ID screen. They can be hard to bring back to life, but can sell for parts, but not for much. Test with coins, rings and pulltabs to see if it works within normal ranges.

When buying waterproof detectors, check the control box and cables thoroughly for cracks or holes compromising the waterproofing features. Moisture or misting showing on the inside of LCD screens is a big giveaway! I would give those a miss, though some might pay a few bucks for a replacement shaft, handle or coil if those were still in good shape.

It can sometimes be worth buying broken detectors as well, as some people will buy them for parts. Again, we need to be very aware of the prices we can sell them for so we can factor our profit margins into whatever we offer for the broken items. Note whether the shaft, coil, handle etc are worth on-selling.

One issue that has cropped up for others, though not yet for me, is the possibility of accidentally buying stolen equipment. I suggest asking for receipts or original packaging where possible if in doubt of the honesty of the seller. If you buy stolen equipment and the police take it, at the very least you lose out on the cash you paid for it. At the worst, you could be charged as an accessory after the crime!

When you're ready to sell the detectors and equipment, post an ad on Gumtree or Craigslist and allow wiggle room in the price for negotiation. Facebook detecting groups are also great for advertising equipment, but check the rules and regulations of the groups as some will allow you to post ads and others won't. Some will only allow ads from people not selling detectors on a regular basis. Ebay is also another route of sale, but is not my favourite due to the fees. Why pay fees when there are so many free avenues of advertising available?

I would suggest nominating a public, well peopled place for transactions, not your home. Especially for high end detectors .. they are rapidly becoming a desirable item for burglars as they're easily pawned.

I found spring and summer the best times to sell, and autumn and winter the best times to buy.

❦ 3 ❦
DETECTOR SERVICE AND REPAIR

I f you're an electronics technician of any sort, this one should be easy for you to add to your repertoire of skills. There are technical manuals available on the internet for many models of detectors, and some metal detector companies will send out manuals on current models if you ask them nicely. This is a niche market - while it may not make you a living, you shouldn't have too much competition. It's a great addition to any other type of electronic repair business. Just make sure your clients are aware any repairs you do are outside of warranty - unless you're lucky enough to get a licence to repair for one or more of the metal detector brands.

4
DETECTOR FRANCHISES

This can be a hard area to make money in, unless you're very good at marketing. The profit margins and turnover can be quite slim. Contact the company manufacturing your chosen brand of detector to find out about becoming a distributor and stocking some of their products. This can work well if you already have a store selling other items, such as a tackle shop or a gun shop. Detectors can be hung on the wall, so they don't take much floor space. Profit margins aren't extensive but if your marketing is spot on, you'll do fine. It's definitely a good idea to join local detecting clubs, as well as online facebook groups involving the hobby.

Another way is to become an Amazon associate and advertise their metal detecting products via your website, facebook page, blog or other social media. This is a very low cost way to get started. Check it out!

5

DETECTOR PERSONAL SHOPPER AND ADVISOR

If, like me, you have acquired a lot of knowledge on detecting and equipment over the years, you can set yourself up as a metal detector personal shopper and advisor. The client can tell you what they want in a detector and you can advise them which detectors suit them the best for those purposes. You can then get them that detecting equipment and put a commission on top. The commission can come from the outlet selling the detectors and/or the client.

You can also flip this and market for businesses selling metal detectors, if they're too busy to do so. This would suit people who are skilled in facebook marketing and virtual assistant type work, as well as knowledgeable about the equipment being sold. This can be an hourly income or a commission based income.

❧ 6 ❦
TRAINING IN THE USE OF DETECTING EQUIPMENT - DETECTING FOR FITNESS BOOTCAMPS

People are always looking for unusual ways to get fit, especially in the springtime. If you have a few detectors, you can set up a special bootcamp in the local parks for a fee (obtain permission from your local council first). This can be a good way to introduce people to the hobby and possibly upsell them to your other services, such as selling detectors, detecting tours and so on. If you have four detectors and have four people in your bootcamp for an hour at $10 each, that's an easy $40 per hour. Don't forget to factor in battery cost or recharging cost. Also, I would suggest asking for a security deposit, refundable at the end of the bootcamp, in case someone does a runner with a detector or one is damaged. Liability insurance is strongly recommended, although it is expensive - some councils expect you to have liability insurance, and others provide it to all park activities.

7
HIRING OUT DETECTING GEAR

Sometimes someone is interested in detecting, but for various reasons hasn't got a detector yet. Maybe they want to try the hobby out for themselves before spending up big? Maybe they're tourists and want to try the nearby gold bearing spots? Maybe they want to try different types of detectors? Maybe they've lost something and want to try and find it? This kind of service can link in well with detector sales or lost item recovery services.

Always take a sizeable deposit and photograph their photo identification and also photograph the hirer themselves.

The deposit is returnable upon returning the equipment in good condition. I used to charge a hourly rate of $20 or a daily rate of $150 plus a returnable deposit to the replacement value of the items hired.

❈ 8 ❈

FINDING NAILS IN TIMBER TO SAVE CHAINSAWS

This service can be conducted with a simple stud finder device from the hardware store .. but only detects nails in logs up to an inch or so deep. Metal detectors can generally detect them up to eight inches deep. Farmers might hire you to detect the trees they want to cut down or cut up for nails or wire that might chew up their chainsaws. This is a service that can link in with many other detecting services you might offer. Charge an hourly rate, and don't forget to ask for permission to detect their land occasionally for fun! Perhaps swap services .. detecting nails and wire in return for detecting permission.

❦ 9 ❦
DETECTING TOURS

Some of you enterprising readers may live in a gold or silver bearing or tourist area. It's worth setting up detecting tours that groups and families can pre book to explore your local areas under your guidance, and use your equipment to find gold, relics or just do some beach hunting. This type of service suits outgoing people who are interested in the history and geology of their local area, and love to share the information in an engaging way while teaching newbies how to use the detecting and gold panning equipment.

❧ 10 ☙

YOUTUBE STORIES AND TUTORIALS

Youtube is a vast how-to and vicarious resource for detecting gadget geeks. We love to watch video after video of all kinds of finds being made with all kinds of detectors. We especially love the how to videos with specific types of equipment. YouTube pays for a certain number of views. If you've got a Go Pro or similar video equipment that you can attach to your head, jacket or detector, you've got a great start.

Next is a simple video editing program on your computer, where you add in commentary, music and captions. Remember, captions greatly increase your views! Many people like to watch videos with the sound turned off. Have a look at other popular detecting videos to see what attracts a large number of views, and pay attention to questions asked in comments to guide you as to what your next video should be about.

❦ 11 ❦
BLOGGING AND WRITING FOR PUBLICATIONS

If you've got the gift of the written gab, this is for you. Treasure hunting magazines are always on the lookout for well written, engaging articles about all aspects of the hobby. Payment varies depending on length of article and whether photographs are included. I personally write on a regular basis for Australian Gold, Gem & Treasure. A decent article with photos will earn me enough to buy my next pinpointer or sand sieve at the very least. Plus it's fun to share information and adventures!

Blogger and Wordpress are great free blogging sites that allow you to add advertisements on the side or below your posts.

I also blog a bit - check out Redback Booth Metal Dectecting on Facebook and Wordpress! Google Adwords and Amazon will allow you to place paying advertisements on the side or below your blog post entry. Make sure advertisements relevant to your hobby are the only ones placed there. Go to Google Adwords and Amazon to sign up and follow their tutorials on how to do it.

If you write a blog entry on a particular subject, you can ensure Amazon places a relevant book or detecting equipment ad right next to the blog entry.

Over time, you might even want to write an ebook on your particular skill set and publish it on Amazon!

❦ 12 ❦
FINDING WAR RELICS OR ARTIFACTS AND SELLING

Living in Australia, this isn't an area I'm very familiar with, but I know that in Europe and the US, as well as other places overseas that are rich in history, metal detecting for war relics or artifacts can be big business. Wherever you may decide to do this, research local laws thoroughly. There are big penalties for illegal digging or removal from the soil of historical items. You also need permission to detect in most historical areas. In some cases, detecting permission is granted, but not digging permission! Not very useful .. make sure the terms and conditions of the permission are properly outlined.

Always be aware of the potential for unexploded ordnance. Don't stab that shovel willy - nilly!

Unexploded bombs and grenades can be a problem especially in fields of war - but I have heard stories of unexploded bombs and grenades being found in ordinary backyards! Dig slowly, carefully and widely whenever possible. Bombs and grenades are usually big signals, so a big signal should equate to a careful excavation.

I f it's fully legal for you to do so, selling found war relics and artifacts can be quite profitable if you hit on a good, productive site. It's worth joining the local historical society or civil war society to find buyers, otherwise there are specialist stores and pawn shops around.

❧ 13 ❧
PROSPECTING FOR GOLD, SILVER, OTHER METALS

If you live in an area known for producing a valuable metal such as gold or silver, it may be worth setting yourself up as a prospector. Skilled prospectors can earn a small living while looking for the next Hand of Faith nugget! Plus they get to see our beautiful land up close and personal.

While decent gold detecting equipment may be expensive, it's usually a one time only investment as most detecting equipment lasts a lifetime and tends to hold its resale value very well. Camping equipment is another expense, but it's the cheapest holiday around if you're bush camping. Kids love it! Just watch out for snakes and drop bears ..

Make sure you have a fossicking licence, and fossicking rights for the area you detect in.

Never detect on private property without appropriate permission. Especially in the bush, if you detect on someone else's legal patch, you're liable to receive a warning shot in your direction from an irate miner.

If you stumble on an old mining camp, there's always the chance that you'll find some old pre-decimal coins and relics as well - always a nice change from prospecting! Plus it indicates there was once gold in the area, and there may yet still be ..

Fossicking is a great way to keep fit too! Those little gold nuggets sure can be buried deep in rock hard soil, and it's a great workout to get it out!

❧ 14 ❦
COLLECTING ALUMINUM AND LEAD FINDS FOR RECYCLING

This may not seem much initially but I used to save all my aluminum and lead finds over a year and then cash in just before Christmas at the scrap metal yard. One year I received over $300 for it all! Save all pull-tabs as well as aluminum cans, and collect those fishing sinkers from the creek bed and the beach. That sure made it easier to buy Christmas presents. If you don't have much room to store them (we have a big shed) then perhaps cash them in a bit more often. Scouts run cash a can drives where you can take bags of cans and pull-tabs to cash them in and help the Scouts at the same time.

If there's a bottle deposit scheme where you are, it might also be worth collecting any bottles you find, and keeping our countryside beautiful!

15

COIN NOODLING, SALES AND COLLECTING

I joined a Facebook group on coin collecting and noodling (looking for collectible coins in a pile of coins is called noodling), and learned which coins to look out for. Not just pre-decimal currency, but also modern coins can be highly collectable and command a decent price. Offset coins, mule coins, mint collector coins, low mintages and error coins can be high in value and worth looking out for in your collection of coin finds on those rainy days you can't get out to detect.

Of course the 1930 Australian penny is the most well known in our country .. it can be valued at anywhere between $15 000 and $50 000 for a circulated specimen. Even a toasted (mutilated by weather and soil conditions) coin would be worth something. Keep in mind there is a lot of fake 1930 pennies out there .. the best thing to do if you do find one, is to take it to a reputable coin dealer for valuation.

Another well known collectible coin worth looking out for is the 2000 Australian $1 mule coin (double rim). Depending on condition, this coin can be valued at anywhere between $300 and $3000. I have seen them priced even higher on eBay!

There's also the 1966 wavy baseline 20 cent coin. Depending on condition, these can sell for between $200 and $400.

Then there's the other holy grails of detecting such as the gold sovereign. Depending on rarity of year and condition, they can sell for between $200 and half a million dollars!

There are many other collectible coins .. far too many for me to list, I'd have to write a whole other book. I'd suggest joining an online coin collecting forum or Facebook group in order to learn best which coins are worth looking out for and selling.

❧ 16 ❧
BULLET COLLECTING AND SALES

Now this is an area that people who fossick and coinshoot in the bush and on farmland might be interested in. It can be annoying to be digging up bullet after bullet when you're looking for something else - but what if the bullets you're digging up are collectible?

There are Facebook groups and online forums dedicated to bullet collecting. The Australian Cartridge Collectors Association is worth looking at for information in this area. Keep in mind that if you collect the bullets and cartridges you find, depending on the state or country you're in, you may need a licence to keep them. It's not always just firearms that are regulated in this way.

If you do happen to find an actual firearm .. it's worth contacting the local police in case it's linked to a crime. Don't worry, if it hasn't been involved an actual crime, you'll get it back. Again, remember the licencing laws in your area with regard to keeping firearms. If your firearm isn't associated with a crime, and is in reasonable condition, it might be worth taking to a firearms antiquities dealer to find out its value and possibly on sell it.

❧ 17 ☙

RESEARCHING AND HUNTING TREASURE CACHES AND HOARDS

This is one of my favorite areas of interest. I haven't found a cache or hoard yet, but now that my children are grown and I can travel a bit more, I look forward to collating all the research I've collected over the years and designing some holiday trips around finding a hoard. I might even write another book on just this subject!

One of the most famous treasure stories located near me is purported to be in or near Byron Bay, NSW. A robbery in 1828 resulted in several boxes of Spanish dollars and Georgian silver coins being buried in one of the North Shore bays after being stolen from the Bank of Australia in George Street. They have never been recovered and are still waiting to be found!

Remember to research the treasure trove laws of wherever you may be searching for treasure. Most countries and states have laws where your hoard must be turned over to the state, though you are paid recompense for the treasure; usually to the value of the entire hoard, or simple set reward.

There are many people out there who find their living by treasure hunting. Quite often those lucky people aren't funded so much by their finds, but by wealthy patrons keen to have their names associated with great historical finds.

A lot of treasure hunters specialise in underwater treasure hunting. Remember the rule, the harder it is to get to where the treasure may be, the fewer people looking for it .. meaning it's far more likely to still be there.

Library research and networking with relevant authorities in historical clubs and academic historians is essential to successful treasure hunting. Local knowledge is a great help, so making friends with locals is definitely useful. For the price of a few rounds of drinks at the local pub, you'll get a lot of possibly conflicting local gossip.

Remember, shorelines change, and in the case of the North Shore treasure, while the loot may have been buried on the beach initially, due to shore movements the loot is now probably miles inland. So a knowledge of historical geology is also very useful! Retroactive satellite maps can help a lot in this situation to extrapolate land movements and geological change over time.

❧ 18 ☙

POLICE FORCE EVIDENCE FINDING

It can be worth popping into the local cop shop and giving them your details as a police evidence recoverist. In most instances if you're called out to a crime scene to detect for guns and bullets and other metal evidence, you'll be paid a consultant fee. This fee varies depending on where you are, the length of time you're working, and who you consult for. The best people to ask are your local law enforcement administration.

19
METEORITE HUNTING AND SALES

Hold onto your hats .. meteorites are worth more than gold pound for pound! They can sell for anything up to $1000 per gram. This hobby ties in well with gold prospecting - you can look for BOTH gold and space rocks.

Keep in mind that not all meteorites are metallic.

Meteorites can be found by the eye on the surface as well as by the detector below the surface. Key indicators that you've found a meteorite are: the rock looks different from surrounding rocks, is heavier than similar sized rocks, and has pinprick holes or pitting caused by gas escaping as it cools after penetrating the atmosphere.

Suspected meteorites can be tested at home with a home testing kit or can be sent to a geologist or meteorite specialist for testing.

20

BEACHCOMBING AND UNDERWATER DETECTING

Now this is a lot of fun. Obviously an underwater detector is required such as a Garrett AT Pro, Makro Kruzer or a Minelab CTX3030. While these can be at the expensive end of the spectrum for detectors, they can pay for themselves many times over in the right hands.

People swim when it's hot and their fingers are swollen from the heat. They get into the comparatively cooler water and guess what, their fingers shrink .. letting their rings loose! Necklaces, bracelets and anklets get torn off by waves. Coinage in pockets comes free.

If you want to go far beyond this kind of detecting, then underwater treasure hunting is a must. There are sunken ships everywhere in the world.

The estimated sunken treasure value worldwide is up to $60 billion.

Even if you're not able to detect close to a known sunken ship location, there is still treasure to be found elsewhere due to storms, currents, seabed upheaval and earthquakes. Moreton Island and other islands in Australia have been known to have the odd Spanish dollar washed up on shore!

21

FIND ART

It's amazing how innovative people can be. I've seen gorgeous necklaces and bracelets made with pulltabs, and bottle top art on canvas. Larger finds have been welded into wild and fantastic creatures, and Harley motorbike models have been created from odd bits of metal found detecting. These items can get a lot of interest at markets and can sell well if you've got artistic ability.

22

INVENTING DETECTING ACCESSORIES AND APPS

There's a clever fellow I know in America who's made a LED light plug for Garrett detectors for those who want to detect quietly at night, or who can't hear due to hearing impairment.

There's some really clever apps out there too designed for detectorists to use. These can bring in mega bucks.

If you're that way inclined, simply find a problem that fellow detectorists tend to have, then come up with a solution, and you'll always get paid!

❧ 23 ❦
MAKING AND SELLING DETECTOR ACCESSORIES

There are detecting accessories that are valued but aren't sold mainstream. For example, ingenious sand scoop designs or specialist toolbelts and belt accessories. The Lesche digger started off as a backyard project and developed into a worldwide business.

Just figure out what you or other detectorists see as a problem, and work out something to solve that problem.

If you have an idea, but don't have the skills to make a prototype, you can go to an engineer to make a prototype and get a patent before you do so on the idea. Kickstarter or other crowdfunding groups are a great financial resource to utilise to develop your idea into a marketable business.

❧ 24 ❧
TALKS FOR LOCAL GROUPS AND SCHOOLS

If you're seen as a detecting expert, or an expert on a specific area in detecting, you may be asked to speak at a club, group event, or school. You can charge a nominal fee for these appearances.

25

SELLING WATCH PARTS FOR NAIL ART OR TO WATCH CLUBS

Sometimes I'll find a watch that's too far gone for repair or is too cheap to repair. In that case, I'll dismantle it and sell the cog parts to a local nail artist for her steampunk nail art, or to a local watch club for parts. This is an infrequent source of income but I love seeing the results of their creative artistry with something I've found.

I hope this book has given you some ideas for generating income from your favourite hobby. Remember to keep it simple, light and fun .. and swing low and slow!

Redback Booth

UNTITLED

DISCLAIMER

The information contained in "Making Money from Metal Detecting," and its components, is meant to serve as a comprehensive collection of strategies that the author of this eBook has done research about. Summaries, strategies, tips and tricks are only recommendations by the author, and reading this eBook will not guarantee that one's results will exactly mirror the author's results.

The author of this Ebook has made all reasonable efforts to provide current and accurate information for the readers of this eBook. The author and its associates will not be held liable for any unintentional errors or omissions that may be found.

The material in the Ebook may include information by third parties. Third party materials comprise of opinions expressed by their owners. As such, the author of this eBook does not assume responsibility or liability for any third party material or opinions.

The publication of third party material does not constitute the author's guarantee of any information, products, services, or opinions contained within third party material. Use of third party material does not guarantee that your results will mirror our results. Publication of such third party material is simply a recommendation and expression of the author's own opinion of that material.

Whether because of the progression of the Internet, or the unforeseen changes in company policy and editorial submission guidelines, what is stated as fact at the time of this writing may become outdated or inapplicable later.

This Ebook is copyright ©2018 by Catherine R. Booth with all rights reserved. It is illegal to redistribute, copy, or create derivative works from this Ebook whole or in parts. No parts of this report may be reproduced or retransmitted in any forms whatsoever without the written expressed and signed permission from the author.

www.ingramcontent.com/pod-product-compliance
Lightning Source LLC
Chambersburg PA
CBHW030514220526
45464CB00006B/2796